Original title:

Budding Licks Along the Witch Pool

Author: Kaido Väinamäe

ISBN HARDBACK: 978-1-80562-412-7

ISBN PAPERBACK: 978-1-80563-933-6

Embrace of the Sylvan Night

In shadows deep, the moonlit glows,
Where ancient trees in silence pose.
A whisper soft, the winds do sing,
Of magic laced in evening's fling.

The stars above like diamonds gleam,
As faeries dance in twilight's dream.
They weave their tales of love and light,
In forest's heart, the spirit's flight.

Beneath the boughs, a secret lies,
In every rustle, every sigh.
The night enfolds with tender care,
As dreams take root in fragrant air.

The brook flows gently, tales untold,
Reflecting moonbeams bright and bold.
In sylvan arms, we find our peace,
As time unwinds and moments cease.

So hold me close beneath the stars,
As magic weaves its hidden bars.
In embrace of night, we shall remain,
As echoes whisper through the rain.

Secrets in the Ripple's Whisper

By the water's edge, the secrets flow,
Where ripples dance and shadows grow.
In every curve, a story wakes,
Of hidden dreams and heartache's aches.

The silver fish, they dart and weave,
Like thoughts unsaid, they tease, believe.
In every splash, a laughter's note,
As willow branches gently float.

The breeze brings forth a lover's sigh,
In twilight's hush, as day waves bye.
The river knows what hearts conceal,
In whispers soft, the truth will heal.

A lantern glows on shores so bare,
And beckons to the brave who dare.
To seek the depths where silence keeps,
The rippling tales that nature weeps.

So let us wander by the stream,
With hopeful hearts and quiet dream.
For in the water's gentle grip,
Are stories shared in love's soft slip.

The Lure of Moonlit Reflections

In silver glow, the night unfolds,
A whisper soft, a tale retold.
The moon's embrace, a gentle sigh,
Where dreams take flight and spirits fly.

Beneath the glow, the shadows dance,
With every glance, a knowing chance.
The water sparkles, secrets weave,
A world of wonders hard to leave.

A silver path on twilight's stream,
Enticing hearts with promises gleam.
In quietude, the magic flows,
As moonlit wonders softly close.

Through glades where ancient stories rest,
The night reveals its hidden quest.
In softly beckoning shades of light,
The lure of dreams takes gentle flight.

Tales from the Hidden Hollow

In quiet vale where secrets dwell,
Lies a tale the breezes tell.
Of whispered lore and shadowed streams,
Where every step ignites sweet dreams.

A gathering of ancient trees,
Their leaves a chorus in the breeze.
The echoes of enchantments past,
In hidden hollow, shadows cast.

Beneath the sky, of golden hue,
Adventures sprout and souls renew.
A tapestry of life and lore,
Where time stands still, forevermore.

With every rustle, every call,
The essence of the magic thralls.
In whispered tales, the spirits sigh,
In hidden hollow, dreams don't die.

Where the Wild Ferns Flourish

In emerald folds beneath the sun,
Where wild ferns weave and stories run.
The earth adorned in shades so bright,
A tapestry of pure delight.

They dance upon the gentle breeze,
A tranquil hymn among the trees.
With every twist, a life anew,
In wild ferns, the spirit grew.

In shaded corners, shadows play,
Where sunlight flickers, bright and gay.
Among the leaves, the secrets hide,
In Nature's heart, they twine and bide.

A haven soft, where moments gleam,
In every breath, a whispered dream.
Where wild ferns flourish, life takes wing,
In gentle arms, the woods will sing.

The Enigma of Water's Palette

In rippling hues, the water glows,
A canvas wrought by nature's flows.
Here colors blend in soft embrace,
Reflecting dreams in fluid grace.

Beneath the surface, stories hide,
An endless depth where secrets bide.
In dancing ripples, shadows danced,
The spirit sways in water's trance.

Each droplet holds a universe,
Of whispered magic, vast and diverse.
In every wave, a tale will rise,
The enigma seen through waking eyes.

With every splash, a voice will sing,
Of hidden realms and timeless spring.
In water's palette, life will flow,
An endless cycle, ever aglow.

Silken Threads of the Evening Mists

In twilight's soft embrace we weave,
Silken threads, the dreams we conceive.
The moonlight dances on the dew,
As shadows whisper tales anew.

The mists arise from deep below,
Wrapping the world in a gentle glow.
Each step we take, a careful tread,
Across the paths where secrets are spread.

A chorus of stars begins to sing,
Of forgotten joys that night may bring.
In this realm where silence reigns,
The heart recalls its hidden pains.

So let us wander through this maze,
The evening mist a silken haze.
For in the night, our spirits free,
Unravel dreams from what will be.

With every breath, the night we claim,
In whispered winds, we find our name.
The threads of dusk, both fine and bold,
Bind every tale that's yet untold.

The Lament of the Wandering Willow

Beneath the willow, shadows sigh,
Its branches droop, as if to cry.
The whispers of the wind do weep,
For secrets buried, buried deep.

Once proud and strong, now bent with age,
A timeless tale, a silent stage.
The roots entwined with earth's own grief,
Breathe heavy thoughts of lost belief.

Yet in the breeze, a memory flits,
Of laughter heard, of happy bits.
The songs of children long since gone,
Echo softly at the dawn.

In the twilight, when the world grows still,
The willow bends to share its will.
A yearning heart beneath the sky,
Calls to the past, a funeral sigh.

So let the rain fall soft and sweet,
To cleanse the ground beneath our feet.
For every tear that nature lends,
Is but a note where life transcends.

Charms Crafted in Twilight's Lullaby

When twilight drapes its velvet cloak,
The world transforms with every stroke.
Charm-laden whispers fill the air,
As magic spins, both light and rare.

With silver threads, the night is spun,
Casting spells as day is done.
In hidden glades where shadows play,
The heart finds peace at close of day.

Crickets hum their evening song,
A rhythm that feels both right and wrong.
As stars awaken, dreams take flight,
Embraced in the arms of gentle night.

Each charm a wish upon the breeze,
Fleeting moments, time's gentle tease.
Crafted from hope and woven with sighs,
The magic lives where the silence lies.

So tread with care on this soft earth,
For every charm has its own worth.
In twilight's lullaby we trust,
As dreams awaken in stardust.

Harmonies from the Hidden Springs

In glades where sunlight meets the stream,
Soft harmonies rise like a dream.
Water sings to stones so worn,
In melodies, pure and forlorn.

Among the branches, whispers flow,
As secrets dance where few dare go.
The gentle rustle of the leaves,
Carries the tales that nature weaves.

A tranquil heart finds solace here,
Where every note is crystal clear.
The rippling patterns weave and spin,
Echoing softly from within.

With every drop, a story stirs,
Of ancient tales and sacred furs.
In hidden springs, life finds its way,
A symphony in shades of gray.

So listen close, the world will share,
The harmonies beyond compare.
For in these springs, our spirits gleam,
Through water's song, we live the dream.

Rituals by the Crooked Creek

In the hush where shadows dwell,
Whispers weave a bold shell.
Ancient oaks bend low to hear,
Secrets shared, both far and near.

Moonlit paths where echoes play,
Rippling waters hold sway.
Gathered souls in quiet grace,
Dancing hopes in tender space.

Flickering lights like fireflies,
Painting dreams across the skies.
Hands unite in solemn tune,
Beneath the watchful, silver moon.

Cloaks of mist in twilight's breath,
Binding life, observing death.
With each chant, the creek conspires,
To feed the heart with ancient fires.

As starlight glimmers on the stream,
Every wish becomes a dream.
From this place where spirits meet,
The world's magic feels complete.

Tongues of Fire in Stillness

In the quiet, embers glow,
Life ignites, then fades to slow.
Flames that dance, they twist and weave,
Spirits rise, yet still believe.

Around the hearth, a circle drawn,
Bonds are forged from dusk till dawn.
Voices swell in whispered tones,
Crackling warmth among the stones.

From the flicker, stories swell,
Tales of wonder, doom, and spell.
Each breath taken, shadows play,
Forming patterns, shaping day.

Mystic echoes catch the air,
Linking futures, dreams laid bare.
Light and dark in sweet embrace,
Time suspended in this place.

With every spark, the heart ignites,
Casting warmth in long, cold nights.
Together, we shall rise anew,
Under the watch of skies so blue.

Beneath the Gaze of the Night-Winged

Through the branches, shadows glide,
Wings of night their silent guide.
With each flutter, whispers weave,
Secrets held that none perceive.

Eyes like lanterns, bright and keen,
Watching over all unseen.
Underneath the starry cloak,
Wisdom speaks, a gentle stroke.

In the stillness, dreams take flight,
Carried forth on wings of night.
Hearts unburdened, spirits soar,
Finding peace on twilight's shore.

Veils of silence, softly spun,
Every shadow kissed by fun.
Nature's dance, a cryptic song,
Beneath the gaze, we all belong.

As the world rests, fears take flight,
Embraced by grace, we see the light.
Together, we shall leave the morn,
And find our solace, reborn.

Charms in the Mist of Dawn

With the dawn, the world awakes,
Gentle magic, softly shakes.
Misty tendrils hug the ground,
In their grasp, lost hopes are found.

Sunrise paints a golden hue,
Brushing life with warmth anew.
Petals whisper, dew-kissed grace,
Nature's spell in every place.

Winds of change begin to stir,
Secrets scattered, lost in blur.
Fingers dance through shimmering light,
Crafting charms in morning's sight.

With each breath, the heart sings loud,
Boundless dreams, beneath the cloud.
In this moment, beauty's wrought,
Life's own magic, dearly sought.

As day unfolds with tender care,
Weaving hopes into the air.
Every whisper, whisper, soft and sweet,
In dawn's embrace, we feel complete.

Twilight's Luring Eye

In the hush of twilight's glow,
Shadows dance with tales untold.
Stars awaken, soft and low,
Whispers wrapped in dreams of gold.

Mist enfolds the ancient trees,
Secrets stir within the night.
A breeze carries every tease,
Of magic lost from mortal sight.

Moonlit paths of silver thread,
Guide the seeker's heart afire.
Step by step, through silence tread,
Chasing visions that inspire.

The Witch's Call of Soft Whispers

In a glade where wild things play,
A witch sings low to the moon.
Her voice twirls like autumn's sway,
In the dark, sweetly opportune.

Leaves gather close to hear her song,
Crickets pause their chirping calls.
The forest knows where hearts belong,
As night drapes softly, like its shawls.

A spell of warmth in every note,
Casts a balm on weary dreams.
On whispered winds, her words float,
Carried by the starlit beams.

Nectar of Bewitched Petals

In gardens where the shadows sigh,
Petals glisten with hidden charms.
Beneath the moonlit velvet sky,
Lies a warmth in nature's arms.

Bees hum soft to nectar's call,
Each sip steeped in love's embrace.
With every bloom, the magic falls,
A fragrant glow, a tender grace.

Dewdrops hide in silken folds,
Whispering secrets of the morn.
Each unfolding leaf beholds,
A tale of beauty, freshly born.

Secrets of the Serpent's Kiss

In the shadows, a serpent lies,
Glistening scales of emerald shade.
With a gaze that mesmerizes,
In stillness, all its games are played.

Underneath the twisted boughs,
A heart beats with an ancient pride.
It knows not of fate or vows,
But of secrets that abide.

With each flick of its shimmering tongue,
It tells stories of olden times.
The whispers of the woods among,
Crafted rhymes in silken chimes.

Murmurs from the Enchanted Abyss

In shadows deep where whispers creep,
The darkness sings, a secret keep.
With tendrils wrought from magic's loom,
A spellbound dance in twilight's gloom.

Beneath the waves of starlit fates,
The echoes call, the night awaits.
With every breath, the moonlight glows,
Unraveling paths where no one goes.

A haunting tune of ages past,
A song that binds, forever cast.
Through crystal tides of fleeting dreams,
The heart finds truth in silent schemes.

In dreams where shadows twist and twine,
A flickering hope, a thread divine.
With whispers soft in twilight's breath,
Awakened souls find peace in death.

So wander close, and heed the call,
In murmurs low, where stillness falls.
For in the depths where magic breathes,
The heart unlocks what fate bequeaths.

The Siren's Embrace in Soft Folds

In twilight's glow, a melody weaves,
The siren's song beneath the leaves.
With whispers sweet, it calls the brave,
To shores where dreams and secrets wave.

With every note, the waters sigh,
A tender lure beneath the sky.
In softest folds of silken waves,
Her voice enchants, and silence saves.

Eyes like stars that dance with glee,
The ocean's heart, forever free.
Wrapped in the warmth of lunar light,
A tale unfolds, both dark and bright.

The crashing waves, a tempest's grace,
While shadows sway in timeless chase.
The siren's embrace, so deep, so wide,
A fragile dream, where fates collide.

So heed her call, the gentle tide,
In every breath, in every stride.
For beauty lies in fleeting sound,
A world awaits, the heart unbound.

Cauldron of Moonlit Dreams

In a cauldron vast, the moonlight pours,
Beneath the stars, the magic soars.
With whispered spells and stardust spun,
The night is ripe for dreams begun.

Brews of wishes, soft and bright,
A swirling dance of shadowed light.
With every stir, new worlds arise,
Reflections caught in dreaming eyes.

Fragrant herbs of ancient lore,
Whisper to us from distant shore.
A potion brewed for boldest hearts,
To weave the night with silvered arts.

In twilight's hold, the world drifts near,
A tapestry of hope and fear.
Close your eyes and feel the pull,
The cauldron's warmth, the night is full.

As stars entwine in cosmic dance,
Embrace the magic, take a chance.
For in the dreams where shadows gleam,
Awaits the truth of every dream.

Echoing Silver Threads of Nostalgia

In whispered tones, the past returns,
Through silver threads, the heart still yearns.
With every echo, a memory weaves,
A tapestry of what one believes.

Through misty lanes of yesteryear,
The laughter lingers, crystal clear.
In twilight's glow, old stories swell,
In every heart, a tale to tell.

Soft breath of time, it lingers long,
In every note, an ancient song.
The world adorned in shades of grey,
Yet in the heart, those colors play.

So dance along the winding road,
With echoes rich, a heavy load.
For in each step, the past does twine,
And through it all, your spirit shines.

Embrace the threads, both worn and bright,
In every shadow, find the light.
The silver strands of what once was,
Unite the heart with whispered cause.

The Magic of the Glade's Caress

In the heart where wildflowers bloom,
Whispers of magic weave through the loom.
Sunbeams dance on the dewy green,
A realm of wonder, quaint and serene.

Gentle breezes stir leaves that sigh,
Soft murmurs echo as dreams flit by.
Creatures of myth peer from the trees,
With secrets held in the rustling leaves.

Stars twinkle bright as the shadows play,
Guardians of night that keep fears at bay.
Embrace the glade's enchanting thrill,
In every corner, there's magic still.

Here wishes are made, with hearts so light,
In the softness of dusk, transforming the night.
Glimmers of hope through branches break,
A promise that dreams are ours to take.

So linger, dear heart, in this sacred space,
Where every step holds a gentle grace.
Let the glade's caress guide your way,
Through the twilight's wondrous play.

Serenade Beneath the Shaded Canopy

Beneath the boughs where the sunlight bends,
A symphony plays, as nature attends.
Leaves fold like curtains, a stage set bright,
With echoes of laughter in shafts of light.

The brook hums a tune, soft and sweet,
Harmonizing with each light summer's beat.
Birds join the chorus, their songs intertwine,
A serenade cast by the whispering pine.

In this hidden realm, the world holds its breath,
Magic unfolds in the stillness of rest.
Joy blooms as brightly as blossoms in spring,
With every note, the forest takes wing.

Time loses meaning in shadows' embrace,
In the heart of the woods, we find our place.
Harmony pulses in the air we share,
An orchestra whispered in delicate care.

As twilight draws near, the song winds down,
Yet the essence of peace will always surround.
A memory cherished, forever to sing,
Under the canopy where dreams take wing.

Reflections in Twilight's Pool

In the stillness where water meets sky,
A mirror of dusk where the soft shadows lie.
Whispers of twilight beckon the stars,
Their shimmering glow, a dance from afar.

The pool holds secrets of night's tender song,
Where ripples play softly, both gentle and strong.
Echoes of twilight, so pure and serene,
In liquid reflections, life's hidden sheen.

Crickets compose symphonies bright,
As moons softly smile, lending their light.
Each twinkle a story from ages gone by,
A glimpse into magic that lifts hearts to fly.

Bridges of starlight cascade through the trees,
Adventures await on the whispers of breeze.
Step close to the edge, let your wishes take flight,
In the heart of the evening, embraced by the night.

Drawn to the surface, dreams all unspooled,
In the depths of the water, our spirits renewed.
Reflections of wonder, we hold them dear,
In twilight's soft pool, where all dreams appear.

The Memorable Fragrance of Dusk

When day's tender light begins to wane,
A fragrant reminder fills the soft lane.
Lavender whispers and roses entwine,
As the sky blurs with hues of crimson and wine.

The earth breathes deeply, exhaling sweet air,
Every scent telling tales of the fair.
Hints of adventure in every soft breeze,
Captured in petals that sway with such ease.

Night's curtain draws close, embracing the land,
With aromas of magic that twine hand in hand.
Violet shadows paint stories anew,
In the lingering fragrance of evening's blue.

As time dances softly on twilight's embrace,
The world finds its rhythm, a gentle pace.
Each gentle whisper, each fleeting sigh,
A fragrance of memories as time drifts by.

So wander, dear dreamer, through dusk's gentle song,
Where scents intertwine, you will always belong.
In the memorable fragrance that fills the night air,
Find solace and warmth, and know we are there.

Whispers of Unseen Magic

In twilight's hush, the shadows weave,
Soft melodies that none perceive.
With every breeze, a secret sigh,
Where dreams take flight and time slips by.

A wand's gentle flick, the air will stir,
Enchantments dance in whispers, blur.
Hidden realms beneath the skin,
Where magic breathes and stories spin.

Among the leaves, the fairies play,
In sparkling glades where night holds sway.
They trace their paths on silken threads,
A tapestry where nothing's dead.

The moonlight spills on ancient stone,
Reflecting tales of those long gone.
The world awakens, softly glows,
As wisps of magic gently flow.

So listen close, to heartbeats near,
In every sound, a tale appears.
For in the still, the truth may sing,
Of unseen magic, held within spring.

Ripples in Enchanted Waters

By the shimmering lake, whispers blend,
Where ripples begin and stories end.
Each droplet holds a world anew,
Reflecting dreams in shades of blue.

The willows weep with tales untold,
In silvered light, their secrets unfold.
Beneath the surface, shadows glide,
Where fish of fortune often hide.

A boat drifts gently, paves the way,
Through velvet night and dawning day.
With every stroke, the magic flows,
In depths where ancient wisdom grows.

Moonlit whispers curl and twist,
In waters deep, no hope is missed.
Catch the reflections, grasp the gleam,
For in this lake, we seal our dream.

So cast your line and take a chance,
For in each ripple, spirits dance.
Embrace the cool, enchantment's fire,
In these deep waters, hearts aspire.

The Cauldron's Serenade

In corners dark, the cauldron brews,
With herbs and whispers, magic stews.
A bubble, a fizz, a flash in the night,
The scent of potions, lessons ignite.

A dash of stardust, a pinch of fate,
In silver smoke, the future awaits.
With each stirring swirl, explosions flair,
Unlocking mysteries hidden in air.

The air is thick with toasty dreams,
As laughter weaves in smoky streams.
Beneath the lid, a world concealed,
In every brew, a truth revealed.

So gather 'round, both old and young,
Listen closely, the witch has sung.
A tale of wonder—potions unfurl,
In the cauldron's heart, enchantments whirl.

For every drop, a spark of lore,
In the cauldron's song, we want for more.
Embrace the night, let magic reign,
In dreams brewed deep, the world we gain.

Secrets Beneath the Moonlit Surface

Beneath the moon's soft silver glow,
Whispers linger where secrets flow.
A hidden world that shadows keep,
In the depths of night, the silence creeps.

The water's edge holds tales of yore,
Of ships that sailed, of legends bore.
Each ripple shimmers with ghostly light,
Where memories drift in endless flight.

The stars above, like watchful eyes,
Guarding the dreams where the old world lies.
In quietude, the night reveals,
The heart of magic that softly heals.

So glance beneath, the surface gleams,
And hear the echoes of enchanted dreams.
In moonlit grace, all fears depart,
For secrets breathe within the heart.

And when dawn breaks, take heed anew,
For every shadow holds something true.
A tapestry woven in night's embrace,
In whispers found, we find our place.

Murmurs of Forgotten Realms

In woods where whispers softly tread,
Ancient tales weave through the night,
Forgotten spirits dance instead,
Underneath the silver light.

Echoes of lost adventures call,
Through the mist and shadowed trees,
With every stumble, every fall,
Awakening the hidden breeze.

Beneath the roots, where secrets lie,
Magic stirs in silence profound,
Flickers of hope in a twilight sky,
Where truths await to be unbound.

In every corner, history gleams,
Glimmers of worlds long since past,
Fleeting like time in fleeting dreams,
Echoes of shadows that linger fast.

So walk with care, let your heart sing,
In realms where the echoes softly play,
Each step is a promise, each breath a wing,
Join the dance of the night's ballet.

Celestial Ripples and Echoing Dreams

Stars above in twilight's grace,
Whispering secrets to the seas,
Galaxies spin in a cosmic race,
Swaying gently in the breeze.

Dreams take flight on luminous waves,
Raindrops glisten like celestial spheres,
Each ripple tells of the paths it paves,
Collecting all our hopes and fears.

With every heartbeat, wonders rise,
Floating soft as a feather's kiss,
In silken shadows of midnight skies,
Awakening memories we miss.

By candlelight, we share our tales,
Of wishes cast on shooting stars,
As time dissolves in mystic veils,
We become all that is ours.

So sway with me, in night's embrace,
Let the universe intertwine,
Together we'll journey through this space,
Towards horizons where dreams align.

Hidden Blossoms in Twilight's Embrace

In the hush of twilight's glow,
Blossoms hide in velvet shades,
Secrets linger where whispers flow,
In the gardens of serenades.

Lavenders and moonlit dew,
Cloaked in shadows, soft and deep,
Their beauty blooms for all who view,
A treasure held in silence steep.

With gentle hands, the night unfolds,
Revealing wonders yet unseen,
A tapestry of dreams retold,
Where magic stirs in leaves of green.

Each petal spins a tale of yore,
Of moments cherished, lost in time,
In twilight's arms, we seek for more,
In nature's dance, our spirits rhyme.

So wander forth where dreams ignite,
A hushed invitation, soft and clear,
Embrace the beauty of the night,
In hidden blooms, your heart draws near.

The Allure of Uncharted Depths

Beneath the waves, a world unknown,
Mysteries swim in shadows dark,
Depths unfathomed, where dreams have grown,
In silence, hidden wonders spark.

Currents twist in a lover's waltz,
Lantern fish flicker in twilight's veil,
Every ripple a tale that exalts,
In this submerged, enchanting tale.

Coral gardens whisper low,
Painting worlds in brilliant hues,
Each creature a story, a graceful flow,
With secrets that the ocean's muse.

As we plunge into the depths of night,
With courage as our only guide,
Let passion spark in the waters' light,
For in the deep, our hearts will glide.

So heed the call of the ocean's breath,
Let your spirit sail on tides,
In the allure of uncharted depth,
Find yourself where the dream abides.

Fantasies Spoken by the Flowing Streams

Whispers of dreams drift through air,
Where silver waters whisper fair.
Sylphs and sprites with laughter sing,
Carried forth on currents' wing.

Beneath the boughs of ancient trees,
Secrets float upon the breeze.
Rippling tales of past and time,
In their bubbles, stories rhyme.

Glimmers of hope in twilight gleam,
Flowing softly, like a dream.
Each stone holds a memory bright,
Sculpted by the moon's pure light.

Sprightly dances in the shade,
Where sunlight dims and shadows wade.
Stream of wishes, bright and clear,
Carving pathways of the sheer.

As the stars begin their play,
The waters hum a lullaby.
Fantasies weave on silken thread,
In liquid voices, joy is spread.

Wildflowers Coursing with Moonlight

In fields where wildflowers sway,
Caressed by night till break of day.
Moonlight bathes each petal fair,
Kissing blooms with tender care.

Colors dance in silver hue,
Whispers shared with skies so blue.
Fragrance spins upon the air,
A fragrant spell that lingers there.

Taking flight on night's soft wing,
Every blossom starts to sing.
With the wind, a secret shared,
All the wild ones, unprepared.

Night descends, a velvet cloak,
While twinkling stars like lanterns stoke.
In this moment, silence reigns,
Earth and sky in sweet refrains.

Through the dark, a promise glows,
A dance of nature, life bestows.
Wildflowers whisper tales of lore,
In moonbeam's light, forevermore.

The Elusive Dance of the Evening Breeze

Eager whispers touch the trees,
In shadows sways the evening breeze.
Softly gliding o'er the land,
A gentle guide, a ghostly hand.

Carrying scents of dusk so sweet,
It weaves a path, where lovers meet.
Twilight's charm, a fleeting trace,
In the hush, we find our place.

Dancing lightly, it seems to play,
In nature's arms, it leads the way.
Feathers of air that softly sway,
Kindling dreams that gently lay.

Beneath the arch of fading light,
It swirls about, a graceful sight.
Elusive spirit, ever near,
Guiding hearts, dispelling fear.

As stars awaken, bold and bright,
The breeze departs into the night.
Leaving echoes of its song,
In twilight's arms, where we belong.

A Tapestry of Night's Embrace

Within the folds of night's embrace,
Dreams cascade like stars in space.
Woven tales of joy and fright,
Chiming softly, hearts take flight.

Moonlit pathways twist and turn,
A tapestry of wishes burn.
Threads of silver, rich and deep,
Weaving secrets, safe to keep.

In this dark, where shadows play,
Echoes of the fading day.
Stories linger on the breeze,
Held in whispers between trees.

Life's complexities align,
Underneath the celestial sign.
Tugging gently at our soul,
As night's embrace makes us whole.

So clasp the twilight, soft and wise,
Let dreams unfurl as darkness lies.
In this tapestry of night's song,
We find the place where we belong.

Echoes of the Misty Marsh

In the stillness where shadows creep,
Whispers linger, secrets deep.
Marshy breath fogs the night,
Reflecting moon's soft, silver light.

Will-o'-the-wisps glide and sway,
Guiding the lost who've lost their way.
Each echo tells a ghostly tale,
Of fae and faery, bright and frail.

Once a dreamer roamed alone,
In every sigh, a haunting tone.
Footsteps dance on squelching ground,
Nature's heartbeat, a lullaby sound.

The reeds rustle with spirits' breath,
Uniting life and whispers of death.
In fog-draped realms, time bends,
Where silence speaks and magic mends.

So linger here, dear wanderer bold,
In hidden wonders, let tales unfold.
For in the mist, a world is spun,
Where dreams are woven, one by one.

The Siren's Song at Twilight

When the sun dips low and shadows grow,
The waves will whisper, soft and slow.
A melody drifts from the foam,
Calling sailors far from home.

Her voice, a lure 'neath a twilight sky,
Bids the restless waves to sigh.
Heartbeats quicken, the horizon blurs,
As night unfurls its silken spurs.

In the deep, where the secrets dwell,
A story carried on a spell.
With every note, a tale unfolds,
Of lost loves and hearts of gold.

Yet listen close, for danger hides,
In beauty's tune, the darkness glides.
Amidst the siren's haunting song,
Lurks the truth that feels so wrong.

So heed the call but guard your heart,
For from her grip, it's hard to part.
In twilight's embrace, dreams often sway,
In the siren's song, the brave may stray.

Shadows in the Bramble Grove

In thickets thick where whispers weave,
Lurking forms make you believe.
Shadows flit 'neath the twisted trees,
Carrying tales on the wind's soft breeze.

Bramble and thorn guard secrets old,
Of ancient beasts and legends bold.
In circles drawn, the moonlight spills,
Revealing magic that stirs and thrills.

Among the roots, a spirit sleeps,
In silence deep, the forest keeps.
Their resin tears, the trees lament,
For kindness lost and time misspent.

While starlight pierces the covered sky,
You'll hear a whisper, a gentle sigh.
A shadow dances just out of sight,
Waiting to whisper its secrets tonight.

So tread with care through the maze so dense,
For each shadow holds a consequence.
In bramble's hold, both fear and grace,
Awaits the journey to a forgotten place.

Mysteries of the Glimmering Stream

Along the banks where willows weep,
A stream weaves tales both old and deep.
Glimmers spark in the dappled light,
Echoing secrets of day and night.

Frogs croak softly in circles round,
The water's laughter, a gentle sound.
Ripples carry whispers of yore,
Each droplet holds a tale of lore.

In silver trails where the minnows play,
Magic stirs at noon and in twilight's gray.
With every bend, the path unveils,
The wonders wrapped in nature's tales.

Yet heed the flow, for it may deceive,
In stillness lurks what few believe.
A glimmer masks the depths below,
Where forgotten dreams and currents flow.

So sit awhile, let the waters speak,
In their embrace, the answers seek.
For in the stream, a truth may gleam,
Awakened softly, just like a dream.

Elixirs of Flora and Fauna

In the glen where the wild blossoms sway,
Petals brew secrets for night and day.
Whispers of herbs in the cool evening air,
Stirring enchantments with delicate care.

Creatures partake in the mystical feast,
Glimmers of magic from greatest to least.
Beneath a mosaic of starlit delight,
Nature's alchemy thrives, silent and bright.

Berries gleam softly, a ruby red hue,
Roots intertwined, ancient wisdom holds true.
Each blossom and bud, a story to tell,
Of ages gone by, in the forest's spell.

Elixirs of life in the moon's gentle light,
Crafting the dreams that awaken the night.
Sipping the essence, a potion takes form,
Healing the heart, in a world so warm.

Harmony in the Stillness of Night

In the hush of dusk, the shadows conspire,
Softly they gather, as stars start to tire.
Melodies whispered on cool, velvet air,
Harmonious secrets dance everywhere.

Crickets are choirs, their song never fades,
Under the blanket of soft, silver shades.
Night flowers bloom with a delicate grace,
Their fragrance a balm, in this tranquil space.

The moon spills her silk through the branches entwined,
Casting a glow that's both gentle and kind.
Dreams intertwine like the tendrils of vines,
Weaving through slumbers where magic combines.

Stillness embraces the world, breath held tight,
While wishes take flight on the wings of the night.
In this cocoon, all the wonders unite,
Painting the sky like a spellbound delight.

The Caress of Shadows in the Glow

Softly the shadows creep into view,
Casting a tapestry woven anew.
With flickering flame, they dance on the wall,
Embracing the night, they whisper their call.

Glimmers of light twinkle bright like a dream,
Fading and merging, a mystical theme.
Each flicker a tale of the day's gentle end,
Where time holds its breath, and the heart starts to mend.

The caress of the dark brings comfort and ease,
A lullaby woven by sweet evening breeze.
In shadows we linger, in secrets we dwell,
Finding the solace of stories to tell.

All hearts are entwined in this soft, tender hue,
Bathed in the warmth that the night gently drew.
It's here in the stillness, we find our own light,
In shadows that cradled the world into night.

Musings from the Water's Whisper

Down by the brook where the ripples play,
Moonlight reflects on the water's ballet.
Each droplet a whisper, secrets unfold,
Casting reflections of tales yet untold.

Nymphs of the stream weave their silken caress,
Serenading the night in enchanting finesse.
Gentle the cadence, as leaves start to dance,
In rhythm with echoes of nature's romance.

Waves of nostalgia wash over the shore,
Carrying memories, hearts longing for more.
In this tranquil moment, our souls intertwine,
Listening closely to wisdom divine.

With every soft ripple, a story is spun,
Of dreams that have passed and those still to come.
The whispering water, a teacher so wise,
Revealing the truths hidden deep in our sighs.

Around every bend, new musings arise,
Reflecting the wonders we see through our eyes.
So linger a while, let the magic persist,
In musings from water, in dreams that exist.

Whispers Beneath the Silver Surface

In twilight's embrace, secrets wait,
Beneath the waves, a quiet fate.
Whispers dance on current's song,
Where silvery dreams gently belong.

Ripples carry tales of old,
Of brave hearts and treasures bold.
The surface shimmers, beckons near,
A world unveiled, free from fear.

Beneath the stars, shadows play,
While creatures of the night sway.
Mirrored depths hide what's divine,
In liquid glass, the realm entwines.

Restless spirits call and sigh,
Through moonlit paths, they softly fly.
In liquid whispers, stories breathe,
With every pulse, new paths we weave.

So venture forth, where dreams ignite,
And secrets pulse 'neath silver light.
For in this realm, as twilight strays,
The heart finds truth in gentle waves.

Fables Carved in Moonlit Waters

Upon the lake, where fables drift,
Moonlit waves, the shadows lift.
Stories carved in rippling sheen,
Echoes brush the night's soft green.

From depths unknown, the tales arise,
Of magic lost, beneath the skies.
Through whispered vows, and promises made,
In the hush, old legends fade.

Each ripple holds a memory dear,
Of laughter, love, and quiet fear.
The moon smiles down, a silver guide,
As dreams and whispers coincide.

Glimmers race across the shore,
Whilst starlit wonders beg for more.
With every glance, life's mysteries blend,
In fables spun, with time to mend.

So linger here, where stories flow,
In moonlit waters, let feelings grow.
For every tale the waters weave,
Is a promise held, a wish conceived.

Secrets of the Enchanted Lagoon

In deep repose, the lagoon lies,
Where twilight meets the starlit skies.
Secrets swathed in emerald hues,
Call to wanderers, beckoning clues.

Beneath the surface, whispers twine,
Of ancient lore and love divine.
With every breeze, a story plays,
Of shimmering nights and golden days.

Tangled roots in the shadowed depths,
Guarding treasures of whispered breaths.
Flickering lights dance and tease,
With the softest sigh of the evening breeze.

Each droplet cradles a lost refrain,
Of fae and dreams, joy and pain.
Through emerald depths, secrets swirl,
Inviting hearts to gently unfurl.

So listen close, let silence sing,
Embrace the magic that shadows bring.
For in the lagoon's alluring hold,
Lies a world where the heart is bold.

Dances of Dusk by the Water's Edge

As dusk approaches, shadows blend,
By the water's edge, whispers send.
The world transforms, all gleaming gold,
In twilight's glow, new stories unfold.

Rippling laughter meets the night,
Where sprites and shadows wrap in light.
With every wave, a dance begins,
As dreams awaken, and hope wins.

Soft serenades from unseen choirs,
Stir the heart with gentle fires.
Around the bend, a secret twirls,
In the soft embrace, the magic swirls.

So linger long by the calming shore,
With every glance, you'll ask for more.
For dusk holds wonders, pure and bright,
In dances sweet, beneath the night.

Embrace the dusk, where stories weave,
With every sigh, the heart believes.
By water's edge, let fantasies flow,
In twilight's arms, let spirits glow.

Enchantment Weaved in Rippling Tides

In moonlight's dance, the waters gleam,
A tale of magic, a shifting dream.
With each soft wave, a story flows,
Whispers of secrets that the river knows.

Beneath the surface, shadows play,
Enchanting hearts, in twilight's sway.
The fish like silver darts do glide,
In depths where mysteries abide.

From pebble beds to banks adorned,
Each corner of this realm is warned.
The breeze that stirs the willows tall,
Carries the echo of nature's call.

As twilight drapes in purple hues,
The tides recite their ancient blues.
With every ripple, magic breathes,
In the spell of water that weaves and weaves.

So cast your gaze upon the tide,
Where enchantments linger, abide.
With open hearts, let wonders find,
The drifting love of nature's mind.

Faint Whispers of the Elder Trees

In ancient woods, where shadows creep,
The elder trees in silence keep.
Their gnarled branches tell the past,
Of whispers echoing, deep and vast.

With knotted roots, they hold the ground,
In sacred spaces, magic's found.
Leaves murmur tales of yesteryear,
Of hopes and dreams that linger near.

Through rustling leaves, the stories sigh,
Beneath the watchful, starry sky.
Each breath of wind, a lover's tune,
With every rustle, an old monsoon.

As twilight falls, the dusk entreats,
To dance beneath the elder's feats.
Ghosts of the past in shadows blend,
A timeless tale, they gently send.

So wander deep where old hearts dwell,
In sacred groves where secrets swell.
With golden light and silver beams,
You'll find the world of whispered dreams.

The Sway of Daisies at Dusk

In fields ablaze with color's cheer,
The daisies sway, both bold and dear.
Their golden faces greet the night,
As shadows blend with fading light.

With gentle grace, they bend and bow,
In rhythms soft, as crickets vow.
The evening draws its lavender sigh,
And whispers softly, time slips by.

Each petal holds the sun's warm glow,
As twilight's breeze begins to flow.
In secret dances, they entwine,
A ballet sweet, by fate's design.

Amongst the blooms, wishes take flight,
On the wings of dusk, they spread their light.
A tapestry of hopes unfurled,
In the gentle heart of a dreaming world.

So lie among the daisies bright,
And weave your dreams in soft moonlight.
For in their sway, you may just find,
A piece of magic, sweet and kind.

Phantoms of the Crystal Waters

In crystal waters, visions glide,
Where phantoms dance and fairies hide.
Reflections twist in ripples clear,
A world enchanted, drawing near.

With every splash, a tale unfolds,
Of mysteries deep, and secrets told.
The surface shimmers with a gaze,
That captures hearts in twilight's haze.

Under the moon, the spirits churn,
In watery depths, their fires burn.
Whispers echo in the night,
With ghostly glow, they take to flight.

In twilight's grasp, where shadows creep,
The crystal waters hold their sleep.
A magic spell that knows no bounds,
In every drop, a song resounds.

So linger near, let wonders weave,
In phantoms' grace, we dare believe.
For in the depths of starlit seas,
Lies the enchantment of ancient trees.

Enchanted Evening at the Water's Edge

The moonlight dances on the lake,
Whispers of magic softly wake.
Ripples twinkle, secrets lend,
A night of dreams that seem to bend.

Flickering lights in the calm air,
Fairy spins, a playful glare.
Beneath the stars, we feel the pull,
Of ancient tales, forever full.

The willow's sway, a gentle song,
Where shadows roam, and night feels long.
In this embrace of serene light,
Hearts ignite, with pure delight.

A breeze that carries sweet perfume,
The night unfolds, dispelling gloom.
Every glance a longing shared,
In this haven, love declared.

Time stands still by the water's side,
In quiet grace, our dreams abide.
Through enchanted moments, souls entwined,
At this edge, the world is kind.

The Ballad of the Hidden Woods

Deep in the woods, a tune does weave,
Echoing tales that none believe.
Mossy paths of shimmering green,
Where whispers hide, and dreams convene.

Under the boughs where silence reigns,
Magic lingers, bound by chains.
Footsteps lead to shadows vast,
Discoveries of a long-lost past.

The creatures speak in riddled rhyme,
Sharing secrets of the time.
In flickering light, a realm unfurls,
A dance of fate in hidden swirls.

Dewdrops gleam on leaves so bright,
Carrying whispers of the night.
Each rustling sound, a ghostly hint,
Of dreams once lived, now gone to print.

So wander here, let wonder soar,
In the embrace of the ancient lore.
A ballad sung by fading beams,
In hidden woods, we find our dreams.

Ecstasy in the Twilight Breeze

As dusk unfolds, a velvet hue,
The twilight breeze brings tales anew.
Softly it kisses the world awake,
A symphony of heartbeats quake.

With every whisper, wishes soar,
Under the glow of stars galore.
A tender touch of evening's grace,
In every breath, find magic's face.

Among the shadows, secrets gleam,
In twilight's fold, we dare to dream.
A dance of light, both near and far,
Guided by the evening star.

Each gust a note in nature's song,
Where hope and longing both belong.
In the gentle hour, we find our place,
Wrapped in love's warm, sweet embrace.

The air is thick with whispered caress,
A moment lost in endlessness.
Ecstasy lingers, sweet and free,
In twilight's grasp, just you and me.

Fen Mystique Beneath the Stars

Upon the fen, the night does sigh,
Beneath a vast and starry sky.
Mist in patterns, soft and fair,
Ancient tales linger in the air.

Golden moons cast shadows long,
Bats flit by with a haunting song.
The water shimmers, alive with dreams,
Where mystery finds its endless streams.

Creak of reeds in the gentle night,
A dance with shadows, a fading light.
Locking gazes with whispering skies,
In the heart of the fen, where magic lies.

Footsteps echo on the silted ground,
In this mystique, our hearts are bound.
Every sigh, a wish on the breeze,
Imprinted moments that will not cease.

So breathe the magic, hold it tight,
In the fen beneath the very night.
A tapestry woven with starlit grace,
In this sacred, enchanted space.

Temptations of a Sylvan Spring

In whispers soft, the blossoms sway,
With honeyed hues and skies of gray.
The brook sings sweet, a siren's call,
Entrancing all who dare to fall.

Each petal hides a fleeting glance,
A promise shared in summer's dance.
The sun breaks through, a golden seam,
And wraps the world in jeweled dream.

But in the shade, a shadow stirs,
A dancing breeze that lightly purrs.
It beckons close, with secrets spun,
To test the heart; is this the one?

The sylvan air, a heady trance,
Where magic waits to take its chance.
Temptation blooms in every nook,
In forest's heart, a fateful look.

Yet caution whispers in the glade,
For beauty oft in darkness laid.
Beware, dear soul, the sylvan charm,
Lest you find it brings you harm.

Echoes of Dappled Shadows

Beneath the boughs, where daylight leaps,
The dappled shadows twist and creep.
They dance along the forest floor,
And whisper tales of days of yore.

In twilight's glow, the colors fade,
As secrets weave a soft cascade.
Each rustling leaf, a gentle sigh,
Echoes of dreams that drift and fly.

A haunting tune begins to swell,
The woodlands hum an unspoken spell.
In crooked paths, the magic thrives,
Encased in heartbeats, hope survives.

Yet caution tugs at every heart,
For shadows play a fickle part.
They lead us far from solid ground,
Where wonder waits, yet danger's found.

In whispers soft, the forest calls,
Beneath its breath, the mystery sprawls.
Embrace the dark, but tread with care,
For echoes linger everywhere.

The Sway of Eldritch Flora

In moonlit glades, the blossoms sway,
With secrets born of night and day.
Their petals whisper ancient lore,
A language lost, forevermore.

With tendrils lit by starlit grace,
They weave the night in soft embrace.
Each shade of green, a story told,
Of wonders born and dreams of old.

Beware the charm of eldritch charms,
For beauty hides in wicked arms.
The blooms may glow with tempting light,
Yet harbor shadows in their sight.

In fragile forms, the magic thrives,
The dance of flora, where danger dives.
With every sway, a heart may yearn,
Each step in faith, a chance to burn.

So wander deep, and heed the call,
For in the night, enchantments fall.
The sway of flora, wild and free,
Could lead to joy or woe, you see.

Shadowed Corners of Twilight Dream

In twilight's grasp, the shadows bloom,
With mysteries creased in silver gloom.
Each shadowed corner, stories sigh,
While dreams unfurl and drift on high.

The world transforms in creeping night,
As stars ignite with gentle light.
Each flicker hides a tale untold,
Of hearts entwined in brave and bold.

Yet in the dark, a caution flies,
For not all dreams wear sweet disguise.
They lure with whispers, soft and low,
As shadows dance in moonlit glow.

Beneath the surface, secrets churn,
And hearts that yearned may slowly burn.
In every sigh, a choice is made,
To grasp the light or be afraid.

So wander forth, but tread with care,
In shadowed corners, dreams lay bare.
For in the twilight's tender seam,
Lies both the love and haunting dream.

The Enigma of the Gloomy Waters

In the depths where shadows dwell,
Secrets murmur, twisted spell.
Rippling whispers, dark and deep,
Awake the dreams that dare to sleep.

Beneath the surface, echoes play,
Lost reflections, led astray.
Ancient tales of sunken pride,
Haunt the currents, never hide.

O'er the waves, a gentle sigh,
As the mist begins to cry.
Fathomless, the waters call,
A beckoning to one and all.

Glittering fish with scales of gold,
Guard the secrets, legends told.
Chilling breezes swirl and weave,
In the hush of dusk, believe.

The moonlit path, a silvery trail,
Guides the brave who dare to sail.
With every wave, a choice to make,
In the gloom, the heart may break.

Threads of Fate in the Thicket

In the thicket where shadows cling,
Weaver's hands dance, fate takes wing.
Twilight glimmers on fragile strands,
Fates entwined by unseen hands.

Whispers rustle through the leaves,
Stories hidden, no one believes.
Birch and bramble hold their breath,
Guarding secrets of life and death.

Footfalls soft on mossy ground,
In the silence, truth is found.
Guided by the echoes near,
Threads of fate draw ever clear.

Each step forward shapes the night,
Casting shadows, dimming light.
In the heart of nature's art,
The web of life can break apart.

Stars above, a distant sigh,
As dreams like fireflies flutter by.
In the thicket, the story waits,
To unveil all that time creates.

Kissed by the Fae's Embrace

In the glen where soft winds play,
Whispers dance at close of day.
Petals fall like fleeting dreams,
Caught in moonlight's silver beams.

Fae with laughter, bright and free,
Invite the heart to stay with me.
Sprightly steps on emerald grass,
Where time and space seem to bypass.

Glimmers found in twilight's glow,
Reveal the magic only they know.
With every heartbeat, the night unfolds,
Stories of love that the heart holds.

Kisses soft like morning dew,
In their realm, the old feels new.
Entwined in joy, lost from sight,
Forever in the soothing light.

Yet when dawn breaks, shadows tear,
From the dream, I wake aware.
But in my heart, their song remains,
A sweet echo of mystic chains.

The Dance of Shadows and Light

In twilight's grip, the dance begins,
Where light meets dark, and hope spins.
Figures flicker like a flame,
In this waltz, we're held the same.

Shadows stretch with gentle grace,
Illuminated by a soft embrace.
Every step, a tale retold,
In the silence, secrets unfold.

Moonlight glimmers, soft and pale,
Weaving spells in night's dark veil.
Every heartbeat echoes near,
Swaying deftly, not a fear.

A symphony of dark and bright,
In every turn, a spark ignites.
Lost in rhythm, souls entwined,
In shadows' dance, the heart is blind.

But at dawn, as shadows fade,
The dance remains, though undisplayed.
Memories swirl in morning's light,
Echoes linger of the night.

The Allure of Stars Eclipsed

In the velvet sky they dance,
Whispers of tales left untold,
Each shimmer a fleeting glance,
Glimmers of wishes foretold.

A curtain of shadow does fall,
Veiling the dreams of the night,
Yet still, they beckon us all,
To chase down the trails of light.

With breath held, we linger and sway,
Captive to magic's embrace,
In twilight's soft, fleeting play,
We find our own secret place.

The moments brush past like a breeze,
Eclipsed by the time's steady hand,
Yet the heart, it yearns and believes,
For the stars will forever stand.

In echoes of silence, we soar,
Boundless as the dreams we create,
The allure of stars calls us more,
As we dance with our fates late.

The Enchantment of Water's Lullaby

Beneath the moon's silver gaze,
Rippling whispers softly sing,
A lullaby hidden in haze,
Where every droplet takes wing.

The brook's gentle laughter weaves tales,
Of secrets held in its flow,
Through meadows and wild, hidden trails,
Where the quietest breezes blow.

Embraced by the cool, sweet embrace,
The world drifts into a dream,
With sparkling reflections in grace,
As light dances on water's seam.

Each ripple, a note, pure and bright,
Cradling fears in its wake,
Guiding lost souls through the night,
With promises never to break.

This enchantment, a song ever dear,
A symphony flowing with heart,
In the hush, we draw near,
As we meld with the magic, a part.

Secrets of the Glistening Ferns

In the emerald shadows they dwell,
Whispering tales of the past,
Secrets entwined, cast a spell,
In emerald cloaks, they are vast.

Each frond a message, a sign,
Of mysteries lost and found,
Beneath the sun's warm, golden line,
In their stillness, wisdom is crowned.

The forests breathe with an ancient grace,
Caressed by the cool, gentle breeze,
In their heart, a sacred place,
Where time flows like whispered leaves.

A shimmer of dew, a glistening dance,
The magic of moments unbound,
In the ferns, we find our chance,
To listen to the world's soft sound.

Guardians of nature's embrace,
Holding the stories so dear,
With each gentle sway and trace,
In their presence, the world feels clear.

Echoes of an Ethereal Clarity

In the stillness of dawn's soft light,
Whispers of worlds yet unseen,
Echoes stir dreams, taking flight,
In glimmers of hope, they gleam.

Through the mist, clarity flows,
As if time pauses to hear,
The silent truth in shadows grows,
Each moment, a memory near.

An elegance dances on wings,
A shimmer of what lies ahead,
With the warmth that soft morning brings,
Promises spoken, not said.

In the quiet, we find our way,
Beneath the arch of the sky,
With echoes that seamlessly stay,
Binding the heart to the high.

Through whispers of light's gentle grace,
We learn of the paths we should take,
In the stillness, we find our place,
In each echo, a new dawn wakes.

The Forest's Breath at Dusk

As twilight drapes the ancient trees,
The forest sighs a whispering breeze.
Shadows dance on the mossy ground,
In the stillness, magic is found.

Fireflies flicker, a soft-spun light,
Guiding the brave through the gathering night.
A chorus of crickets sings in delight,
Nature's embrace feels just right.

The moon peeks through a tangle of leaves,
Casting dreams where the heart believes.
Each rustle tells of secrets untold,
Woven in tales of the wise and bold.

Beneath the boughs, where the wild things roam,
Every creature finds its home.
The air is thick with an old, sweet song,
Where the heart beats fast, yet time feels long.

In the forest's breath, we explore and trust,
Mapped by starlight to wander, we must.
With every step, a spell is spun,
In the dusk of the day, our journeys begun.

Mirage of the Whispering Glade

In the glade where the silver ferns sway,
Mysteries linger from yesterday.
Sunlight filters through branches high,
Bathed in whispers of the softest sigh.

Echoes of laughter from spirits near,
Weaving through willows, so crystal clear.
The air shimmers with colors unseen,
A canvas of dreams where we have been.

The brook giggles over the stones so light,
Playing hide-and-seek with the fading light.
A mirage dances on the water's face,
Inviting the wanderer to slow their pace.

Each flower blooms with a tale to spin,
Of laughter, of loss, where shadows begin.
In this realm, the ordinary fades,
Magic awakens in sunlight's cascades.

So linger awhile, in this sacred space,
Where time slips softly, a warm embrace.
Let the glade cradle your restless heart,
For here, dear friend, is where dreams start.

Secrets Woven in the Currents

In the river's rush, secrets lie deep,
Whispers of history, their promise to keep.
Beneath the ripples, tales intertwine,
Of those who dared, of the brave and divine.

Each leaf that floats tells a story untold,
Of lovers, of wanderers eternally bold.
The water glistens, alive with a dance,
Inviting the curious to take a chance.

As twilight descends, the world fades away,
Mirrored reflections of night and day.
Every splash holds a memory's trace,
In the flow of the water, we find our place.

The currents hum with a wisdom profound,
Echoes of voices from the lost and found.
If you listen close, you might just hear,
The tales of the past, both distant and near.

So heed the river, a guide so wise,
In its winding path, true magic lies.
For in its embrace, the heart can find
The secrets woven, forever intertwined.

Glimpses of a Forgotten Realm

In the shadows of dreams, a realm unfolds,
Where the stories of ancients glow like gold.
Haunted by time and enchanted by grace,
Each corner conceals a familiar face.

Walls of ivy cradle the past so dear,
Echoes of laughter, a song to hear.
Through the gnarled branches, the light breaks through,
Painting the world in vibrant hues.

The air is thick with a scent of the wild,
As whispers of magic beckon like a child.
Each step reveals wonders, forgotten and lost,
In the heart of the realm, across cosmic frost.

Through hidden doorways and overgrown trails,
Life thrives in secrets, where adventure prevails.
With each gentle breeze, a tale is set free,
Of heroes and creatures, of you and me.

So venture forth, let the journey ignite,
In this forgotten realm bathed in starlight.
For the magic within is a treasure untold,
Waiting for hearts brave enough to be bold.

Yonder Beyond the Velvet Veil

In shadows deep where whispers sing,
A world awaits, a wondrous thing.
Through velvet veils the secrets seep,
Where time stands still and dreams do leap.

The stars above like eyes that gleam,
Reflecting every blissful dream.
With every step, the unknown calls,
As mystery in silence sprawls.

Dare you traverse this hidden land?
To walk where few have dared to stand?
In twilight's hush, new tales arise,
And truth unveils in softened sighs.

Awake the magic, feel the thrill,
Beyond the veil, your heart will fill.
In realms of wonder, fate entwined,
A journey waits for those who find.

Through labyrinths of light and shade,
The heart's own north, the dreams we trade.
With courage bold, let spirits soar,
For yonder holds forevermore.

The Soft Glow of Phantom Flowers

In moonlit glades where stillness sighs,
Phantom flowers bloom and rise.
Their petals soft, a ghostly hue,
Whispers of dreams that once flew.

Beneath the stars, they sway and dance,
In twilight's spell, they take their chance.
With fragrant breath, they paint the night,
A symphony of soft delight.

Each bloom a tale of love and loss,
A fleeting gift, a gentle gloss.
For in their glow, the secrets nest,
Of moments cherished, dreams expressed.

When dawn awakens, they will fade,
Yet in our hearts, their scents are laid.
A memory sweet, a tranquil power,
Forever kept, this phantom flower.

So wander close, let spirits weave,
In gardens where the night believes.
Embrace the glow, feel heartbeats thrum,
Among the dreams that softly come.

Reflections of a Shimmering Secret

In waters clear, where secrets dwell,
A shimmer speaks, a magic spell.
Beneath the surface, stories glide,
As moonbeams dance on currents wide.

Each ripple holds a whispered truth,
Of ancient tales and fleeting youth.
With every glance, a story unfolds,
In liquid mirrors, the heart beholds.

So lean in close, and dare to see,
The shimmering depths of mystery.
In tranquil pools, reflections sigh,
Of dreams that weave between the sky.

With every wave that breaks the still,
A pulse of life, a fleeting thrill.
The world beneath holds endless grace,
A shimmering secret, time will trace.

In this embrace of dusk and dawn,
Where hopes arise and fears are gone,
Beneath the veil of silvered light,
Reflections bloom in spiritual flight.

Enchanted Echoes of the Water's Dance

By the waterfront, where willows weep,
Enchanted echoes cradle deep.
In rippling measures, dreams are spun,
Where laughter meets the setting sun.

The waters sway in joyful grace,
Reflecting magic in every space.
As breezes weave through twinkling trees,
A melody rides upon the breeze.

With every splash, a story shared,
Of wishes dreamed and souls laid bare.
In tranquil tides, the heartbeats throng,
As nature hums an ancient song.

Take heed, dear friend, of waters' sway,
For echoes whisper what hearts convey.
In every ripple, secrets glean,
A dance of stories yet unseen.

So linger long where waters meet,
In rhythmic pulse, let spirits greet.
For in their dance, our dreams align,
Enchanted echoes, forever shine.

Flowers of Incantation

In the glade where whispers bloom,
Petals sing a soft, sweet tune.
Each color holds a magic spark,
Illuminating shadows dark.

Beneath the moon's enchanted gaze,
Flowers weave their secret ways.
Dewdrops catch the twinkling light,
Transforming dreams into the night.

With every sigh, a spell is spun,
In moonlit dance, the night has begun.
Roots entwined with lore untold,
A tapestry of ages old.

The air hums with ancient lore,
As blossoms bloom, forevermore.
With every breeze, they call and sigh,
In this realm where wishes fly.

So tread with care on paths unseen,
Where magic lives in shades of green.
For flowers speak in language rare,
And weave their spells in fragrant air.

The Allure of Hidden Currents

In twilight's glow, the waters sway,
Beneath the stars, they dance and play.
Ripples whisper secrets deep,
Inviting hearts to wake from sleep.

Currents twist through shadowed dreams,
Where nothing is as simple seems.
A journey into depths unknown,
Where ancient tales have softly grown.

With silver threads that swiftly glide,
Mysteries in the depths reside.
The call of depths, a haunting song,
That lures the brave to venture long.

In every swirl, a story weaves,
Of hope and wonders one believes.
The surface masks what lies beneath,
A world enshrined in woven sheathe.

So cast your thoughts upon the stream,
Let dreams emerge, like fleeting beam.
For in the currents, life does dwell,
With whispers 'neath the waving swell.

Songs of the Forgotten Grove

In a grove where shadows lean,
Echoes of the past are seen.
Trees hold whispers, soft and low,
Tales of youth in twilight's glow.

The air is thick with magic's breath,
A realm untouched by time or death.
Each branch a tale of lore and fate,
In twilight's hold, we meditate.

The songbirds weave a lullaby,
For wanderers who dare to try.
With every note a memory sighs,
Of laughter lost and love that flies.

Through tangled roots and emerald hue,
The grove unveils its secrets true.
Inviting souls to pause and reflect,
In harmony, their hearts connect.

So linger here, O traveler bold,
In this grove of magic untold.
For every glance, each rustle near,
Holds a song that time won't smear.

Dances of the Sylphs and Sprites

In the twilight where shadows flit,
Sylphs and sprites in moonlight sit.
With laughter light, they weave and play,
Invisible guests of dusk and day.

Their laughter dances on the breeze,
A melody that stirs the trees.
In every flicker, magic glows,
As through the air their spirit flows.

Glimmers of mischief, joy, and grace,
They spin the stars in their embrace.
With swirling skirts of mist and light,
They paint the heavens with delight.

In every twirl, a spell is cast,
Unraveling the futures vast.
They beckon dreams from slumber's hold,
As stories of the heart unfold.

So close your eyes and feel the night,
Join their dance of pure delight.
For in their world of shimmering flight,
Magic breathes beyond the sight.

The Spell of Nightshade Blossoms

In the garden where shadows creep,
Nightshade blossoms silently weep.
Their dark petals whisper low,
Secrets only the moonlit know.

With each breath of the midnight air,
A haunting charm that fills the lair.
Beware the allure of their song,
For enchantments can lead us wrong.

The scent of magic lingers near,
Wrapping the heart in a shroud of fear.
In twilight's grasp, they swiftly bloom,
Filling the world with a sense of doom.

Yet under the stars, they softly glow,
A reminder that beauty may hide our woe.
Dare to tread where darkness lays,
And dance with shadows that softly sway.

So take care, wanderer, in the night,
The spell of nightshade can feel so right.
Yet in each blossom is a choice to make,
A path to take, or a heart to break.

Haunting Melodies from Verdant Shores

The waves weave songs upon the sand,
Whispers of dreams from a distant land.
With each crest and fall they play,
Haunting melodies at close of day.

Seagulls soar on the salted breeze,
A dance that sways through ancient trees.
The rhythm calls, a siren's call,
Echoes of nature that cradle all.

In twilight's hush, the world stands still,
As mystery blankets the rolling hill.
The sea reflects the twilight's hue,
A canvas painted in shades of blue.

With every note, the heart takes flight,
Unraveling threads of stars at night.
The verdant shores, a sacred place,
Where time forgets its restless race.

So listen close to the waves' embrace,
In haunting melodies, find your grace.
For nature sings in whispers sweet,
To guide the weary, lost on their feet.

The Lush Breath of Hidden Places

In the woods where shadows gather,
Life breathes slow, with gentle lather.
Moss carpets floors of emerald green,
Whispering tales of the unseen.

Dappled sunlight, a painter's brush,
Through branches sways, creating a hush.
Every rustle, a story to tell,
Of deep woods where secrets dwell.

Hidden paths through the twisted glade,
Where dreams are spun and memories fade.
The lush breath carries a fragrant kiss,
Inviting all to wander, to miss.

With each step further, the heart beats wild,
In nature's arms, like a fearless child.
The hidden places whisper still,
Calling forth hope with every thrill.

So delve into realms where the wild hearts roam,
And find in each breath your peaceful home.
For in the lush depths, life's magic waits,
Unlocking the dreams that destiny creates.

Whimsies of the Murmuring Brook

By the brook where the willows lean,
Lies a world soft and serene.
With every ripple, a playful wink,
In glistening waters, thoughts drift and think.

The whispers of water weave through trees,
A melody carried on the breeze.
Each stone cradles stories anew,
Whimsies of nature, so bright and true.

The brook dances with laughter and glee,
A tapestry of joy for all to see.
Beneath the surface, the secrets glide,
In playful currents that twist and hide.

Dragonflies flit, like jewels in the sun,
Their graceful ballet, a dance just begun.
In this haven where waters sing,
Every moment feels like spring.

So linger awhile by the murmuring flow,
Let your heart learn what the waters know.
For in the delights of this gentle brook,
Are whispers of life, in every nook.